Social Media Marketing 2019

Advertising Guide for Your Business on Instagram and Facebook

Table of Contents

Introduction

Social media marketing is a form of digital marketing which allows users to create and share content on different social networking sites with the aim to achieve business-specific branding and marketing goals.

It is impossible to bracket social media marketing into a small equation since it is a broad field that covers various dimensions of social media platforms. It is also a very powerful tool for businesses that want to expand their services by reaching out to potential customers on the internet.

After all, your target audiences are already out there, interacting with brands. What's your stance on it? Shouldn't you be out there as well to get potential clients by showing them what they want to see? Social media marketing is your way to reach those people who aren't on your customer base and does not know about your business. If you are not using different social media platforms, predominantly Facebook, Instagram or Twitter, then you are missing out a lot. Planned social media marketing campaigns with focused audiences, targeted demographics, and interests work like a charm. Businesses can generate leads through targeted ads supported by well-articulated content and visuals.

Before starting off with campaign planning for any of the social media platforms, you need to answer some basic questions, including:

- Which social media platform would work best for your business?
- What is the purpose of your social media marketing campaign?
- What is the ultimate goal that you want to achieve through the social media marketing campaign?
- Have you decided on your focused audience?
- Have you set any milestones to achieve the final goal?
- Which content type will you use to promote your brand's products or services?
- What type of message do you want to convey to your audiences?

Once you are all set, you will be able to create your social media marketing campaigns in a better way. If you want to compete with other brands in the industry, then it's time for you to learn the tactics of social media marketing and how it can help you reach the right audience. In this book, you will learn about the top trends of social media marketing strategies for Facebook and Instagram, which will ultimately grow your client base.

2019 is here, and it has proved to be an impressive year for brands in terms of marketing and advertising. However, nothing comes easy. Gone are the days when brands use to maintain passive engagement with the followers, let it be on Facebook, Instagram or Twitter. If your brand is unable to keep up a conversation with your audiences 24/7, you can consider yourself out of the marketing game. To sell products or services, your business needs to adopt "real-time engagement" by maintaining conversations with users. New users want to be involved, listened to, and appreciated. To understand the dimensions, criteria, and tactics of audience engagement, further sub-division of each aspect is explained in the next chapters.

Chapter 1: Marketing on Facebook

Facebook is a great social media platform which is widely used by brands for the promotion of their products and services. Facebook marketing can help you win potential users across the globe. It consists of many connecting dots that allow the successful creation and execution of a campaign. Undoubtedly, Facebook is one of the most casual and easy-to-use platforms that has given businesses and consumers a chance to interact with each other. People prefer to buy online products instead of visiting stores, after all. Thus, entrepreneurs can sell their products to such customers.

Successful marketing on Facebook requires a well-drafted social media strategy. However, there are certain aspects that you should keep in mind before jumping into the Facebook marketing campaigns. To further understand the depths of advertising and associated techniques related to it, a further breakdown has been done to understand the importance of each feature separately. This will help you in understanding different aspects of marketing and branding on Facebook. Let's dig in and see what Facebook has to offer in 2019 for all the businesses out there.

Personal Branding on Facebook

Facebook is a very powerful instrument for personal branding as it has over 200 million active users.[1] Sharing online enables you to build a virtual identity, which reflects your professional and personal brand. Without any boundaries or restrictions, you can connect with thousands of valuable connections. Nevertheless, managing an online persona is extremely difficult. Without the proper control mechanisms, building a social and professional image appears to be nearly impossible.

Socrates said 2400 years ago, if you want to gain a reputable image, then work hard for what you desire. Therefore, personal branding through Facebook has always been considered as a luxury reserved only for big entrepreneurs and famous people in the past. Now, though, anyone who wants to become popular can use Facebook for personal branding.[2]

---

[1] Logan, B. (2009). 200 million strong [Blog Post]. Retrieved from https://www.facebook.com/notes/facebook/200-million-strong/72353897130/

[2] Petruca, I. (2016). Personal branding through social media [PDF File]. Retrieved from

So, how can you exactly create a personal brand on Facebook in 2019? Below are some of the top points that you should consider for elevating your brand.

Plan Your Branding Strategy

It is important to understand your audience type before brainstorming for your branding strategy. You will only be able to devise an effective plan for your business after that since most people create an affiliation with a brand's name and their established credibility. To gain users' trust, building a successful brand name must be a prime concern. Set goals and make a future plan on how are you going to implement your branding strategy, e.g., brand awareness, improved website traffic, and ranking on top of search engines by using the SMART technique.

Then, pinpoint the audience you are going to target in the market of competitors, e.g., marketers, coaches, gamers, business developers, graphic designers, or anyone else who can be relevant to your brand on Facebook. Nowadays, people focus more on quality content, so it's better to run ads on posts that are vibrant and creative. For example, if you own a local clothing shop, you would want to target the users near your place. You can do this by customizing ads that will only be shown to the people of that locality. Such funnel-approached advertisements will generate leads and bring more sales to your brand.

The final step is to keep track of the progress of your branding strategy on a daily basis. You can do so through Facebook Insights. Once you have the analytics and insights of previously promoted posts, you can use that data to extract key points. This will enable you to improve your future ads by incorporating elements that worked well for the previous posts.

Pro tip: Make sure to add your store on Google My Business app to enhance its visibility on search engines.

Brand Identity and Brand Positioning

There's a large pool of potential customers that you can reach on Facebook. This happens when you provide important business information on your page by using brand keywords. Sharing such details will make it more professional and attract potential customers. You can either use hashtags or link your Facebook page to Google My

http://ijcr.eu/articole/345_10%20Irina%20PETRUCA.pdf

Business.

People use Facebook for social activities, engagement, real-time interaction, and even shopping. Considering the importance of digital marketing and online shopping, brand positioning has become an important feature to market yourself, your business or your brand. Adopting the right social media strategy with clear goals - e.g., generating leads, increasing followers or selling goods on a Facebook page or a website - can create a pleasant image of the brand in users' minds. You have to focus on providing synced information on all your social media profiles. You will also have to enter the same business hours, location, and other brand information everywhere to be able to target the right audiences across the web.

Real-Time Engagement on a Daily Basis

User engagement on Facebook has to be related with your personal branding strategy, motivational quotes or industry-related trends done through posting on your profile, page or group. It allows you to connect with people on a personal level.

Sharing posts that create engagement is essential to make a user want to show interest to a brand. The use of questions to asks for their feedback makes them feel involved and appreciated as well. This is an important aspect to consider in the consumer-based community. For example, if someone leaves a comment on any of your posts or sends you direct messages using Messenger, make sure to respond instantly rather than leaving it to automatic answers. This step is of significance because the customer believes in the authenticity of your brand. Also, continuous engagement and trust can only be developed through non-stop interactions with them.

Use of Facebook Stories

It is important to understand the functionality of Facebook Stories. The significance of each aspect of this feature are explained below in detail.

What are Facebook Stories?

Facebook Stories was introduced in 2017. The idea was originally adopted from Snapchat, which later modified its version a bit. Facebook has more than 1.8 billion users. The launch of Facebook Stories didn't create much hype at that time. However, a recent survey revealed that it started to pick pace and was able to receive 150 million views per day.[3] In 2019, Facebook Stories will reshape the future of videos and social media marketing. Marketers will be able to increase their sells by using some of its great features.

Stories posted on Facebook basically consist of images and short videos that last for 24 hours on the top of your newsfeed. These are smart tools to engage your audience in your services or products. With the changing trends in the social media industry, videos, in particular, are set to be the next rising trend. Companies are already benefiting from it, to be honest. Facebook Stories is like another portal for your online presence in which can share real-time activities that you want to promote. The photos and clips posted there are undoubtedly engaging, immersive, inbound, inherently social, and creative.

Interactions through Facebook Stories

The right content shared with the right audiences at the right time will always help in creating an emotional bond with them. Consider yourself as a brand that sells baby products. Now, how would you want to advertise them: through unattractive monotonous videos or by adding a real baby to your video with a blend of an emotional message to it? When you think of the human thought processes, emotional belonging plays a vital role in buying goods. Thus, if you will target the audience by creating a baseline of heartfelt message, chances are that you will be able to sell your products to the right market.

Facebook Stories is yet another delightful way to present your customers with visually appealing content. The right video uploaded through this trending channel can help in creating face-to-face interactions and intimacy with consumers. If you want to make an everlasting brand story for your audiences and achieve a benchmark, then utilizing an interactive platform like Facebook can give you your best shot. After all, it supports approximately 2.23 billion users daily.[4]

Now that we know what Facebook Stories is and how interactions can be established using this medium, the real question: how can marketers take advantage of Facebook Stories to promote their brands?

---

[3] Constine, J. (2018). Facebook Stories: The complete guide for businesses in 2019. Retrieved from https://www.oberlo.com/blog/facebook-stories-guide

[4] Statista. (n.d.). Number of monthly active Facebook users worldwide as of 4th quarter 2018 (in millions). Retrieved from https://www.statista.com/statistics/264810/number-of-monthly-active-facebook-users-worldwide/

Advantages of Facebook Stories

Facebook Stories are the talk of the town these days. Brands around the globe are shifting to this feature for better engagement and leads. This feature is primarily popular because of two essential things: storytelling and video-sharing capability. A combination of both makes it a perfect platform for audience engagement and brand growth.

There are some prominent advantages of Facebook Stories, though, that you can get hold of to increase brand awareness, sales, and user engagement.

1. Focus on making time-sensitive and creative content

One of the many things that distinguishes Facebook Stories from other applications is the fact that it offers momentary information. Different brands take advantage of users' social anxiety, which is referred to as FOMO - the fear of missing an important news or detail on social media.[5]

As a brand owner, you understand the importance of what your followers want to see and read. Most of the social media subscribers want to stay updated about new offerings and trends that they care about. This is where you stand a chance to captivate your users' attention by creating content that not only matters to them but also does not take much of their time. To be specific, you can use Facebook Stories to:

- **Give a personal touch.** Let your followers see what goes behind the scenes and show them your office or how your company makes certain products. Allow them to feel involved so that they can relate to your brand.
- **Let the world know about you.** To grab the attention of the audience, brands can make sure to announce their special deals, discounts or upcoming products. This will help in boosting the brand image and would gain more popularity.
- **Offer competitions.** What do your engaged followers get in return? Do they get any loyalty points or rewards for their brand loyalty? It is important to reward your loyal followers by hosting competitions. This would allow brands to create a healthy user-brand relationship.

2. Be your own kind

Facebook and Instagram stories are synced, but it doesn't mean that you should share the same content on both platforms. This will only make your followers lose interest in your brand. Each social media channel, after all, has its own working mechanisms. If

[5] Hobson, N. (2018). The science of FOMO and what we're really missing out on. Retrieved from https://www.psychologytoday.com/us/blog/ritual-and-the-brain/201804/the-science-fomo-and-what-we-re-really-missing-out

you think more deeply about these platforms, though, Instagram attracts more engagement on stories than Facebook. Your followers want to see fresh, creative, and new content. This is where you can play smart by using the same content and presenting it in different forms by revamping the design format or text. Think about your audience, their likes and interests, and then craft a story around them to attract Facebook users.

3. Stay focused on your brand

Facebook stories have their own unique filters that brands can use. These features can be utilized by turning on the effects mode that will appear on the screen. You can add different objects such as texts, stickers, lighting, and other components. Such things can highlight your brand's image and convey your message in a creative way.

Furthermore, it allows you to boost brand awareness by:

- Staying consistent with certain filters to stay aligned with the brand's image;

- Adding relevant themes to enhance the brand's visual representation and running promotions; and

- Using unique font/text styles to match the story.

4. Offer Memorable Experiences

Customer satisfaction is a significant source of concern in the world of social media marketing. To enhance their experience, Facebook Stories is a great tool to use. It lets you build your advertising and content strategy in a more enhanced way. For instance, if you are planning to host an event, you can involve your followers by showing them visually appealing videos that will encourage them to sign up for it. Alternatively, you can share a miniature recording of the people who are behind the upcoming meeting create curiosity among Facebook users.

Another way to promote your event or new announcements is through collaborative Facebook Stories. This allows you to share and cover your stories from every possible angle. To be specific, brands can connect their stories with other people's creations within their network. It's an effective way to improve your brand's presence and user engagement.[6]

5. Think beyond Promotions

---

[6] Hutchinson, A. (2018). Facebook rolls out group stories to all regions. Retrieved from https://www.socialmediatoday.com/news/facebook-rolls-out-group-stories-to-all-regions/543562/

Considering you already have a perfectly designed social media strategy, remember that there is always more to your social media presence. It is not just about promoting posts or getting leads and page likes. As a brand owner, you need to focus on offering more engaging content to your users. While your followers want to see new products and trends, they also want to know about the people behind a certain label. Emotional connection is the core of all brands; thus, if your company gets to develop that connection with its followers, then your may consider it as a jackpot.

Rather than merely focusing on increasing your monthly sales, it is important to invest on content that is both informational and delightful for your targeted audience. As a sensible and customer-oriented brand, you can do it by:

- Celebrating business achievements and new customer-focused products announcements;

- Showing previews of upcoming projects or goods;

- Sharing exclusive clips of relevant events related to your brand;

- Providing fact-based content for your audiences; and

- Sharing relevant tips related that can eventually help the users to learn something out of them.

Facebook Stories for CTAs

Facebook recently added a new call-to-action (CTA) feature to Facebook Stories for marketers. It makes it easier for businesses to direct their audience to a particular landing page and further interact with them. The currently available CTAs are "Call Now", "Get Directions", "Learn More", "Book Now", and "Shop Now". If you plan to promote a certain product or want to direct your audience's attention to a particular promotion, for instance, you now have a CTA to add for either. Viewers can see your CTA within your stories and can slide up from bottom of the screen for further interaction.

Importance of Transparency for Brands

We have discussed the importance of social media and its role in people's lives. Platforms like Facebook and Instagram are great tools for building a brand-audience relationship. There are thousands of pages on these channels that continuously share information with their followers, but can they commit to the authenticity of such content? After the release of the General Data Protection Regulation in May 2018, businesses around the world have become more considerate about being transparent in terms of processes and information they share. If you want to increase brand loyalty like other brands , then adding the transparency factor can do the work since people want to believe in what they see on social media.

Marketing Charts released nine vital aspects of transparency to help brands understand the importance of transparency.[7] Brands need to pace up their game to meet the transparency standards on social media platforms. The concept has become the baseline for all the businesses out there, after all. In today's age, users have become more considerate about the authenticity and transparency of the content.

Recently, a study was conducted on a sample of 1000 US-based customers to understand the psyche behind their beliefs, trust, desires, and expectations towards their favorite brands.[8] The investigation revealed the following results:

- About 86% of consumers believe that lucidity plays a major role in building a strong trust-based relationship. The presence of transparency in brand's strategies and processes can assure a long-term loyalty from customers.

- Social media demand for clarity, which may create challenges for the businesses but still offer long-term rewards. This is indicated by approximately 40% of the people who believe in benefits of overall transparency regardless of attribution with social media.

- Brands have extensive margin in creating and expanding transparency measures across all of their social media accounts. About 81% of the digital users believe that brands need to step up by taking responsibility on the authenticity of the content that they share on different platforms.

How Do Brands Ensure Transparency?

As a brand, you should first ask yourself a few questions. "Why should someone support my brand or become a follower when others are offering the same kind of services?"

---

[7] Marketing Charts. (2018). So people want brands to be more transparent on social media. What does that mean? Retrieved from https://www.marketingcharts.com/brand-related-105434

[8] Sprout Social. (n.d.). Social media & the evolution of transparency. Retrieved from https://sproutsocial.com/insights/guides/

"Am I any different from my competitors?" "What makes my brand unique?"

In order to become transparent on social media, there are few things that you should consider as a brand owner.

1. Infuse the brand's personality into what you share

Personality plays a major role in distinguishing one person from another. There are some unique traits that make them stand out in a crowd. Take your brand as an individual entity that you want to promote on the basis of its unique personality traits. Infuse your brand's character into the products that you sell or the services that you offer. This will help you in gaining the trust of your audience.

2. Tell your audience about the brand's aspirations

It doesn't matter whether you have a clothing brand, an e-commerce shop or even a bakery. You must have an aspiration - a goal that you inspire you to deliver to the consumers. You can use visuals, texts or videos to share your brand's aspirations with the latter to ensure having a sense of relatability among the users when they see you sharing your brand's story.

3. Share your stance as a brand

You will need to share the timeline of your brand if you want to get your audience hooked to an upcoming product or a discount announcement, as well as if you wish to maintain the engagement rate on your social media pages. Sharing your struggles, achievements, and fallbacks can ensure your label's transparency.

Your followers will feel motivated to connect with you more upon knowing that the brand that they are interacting with and investing in isn't merely a brand. There is more to it than what meets the eye; it promises to unfold untold stories and provide an unforgettable experience. To make that happen, therefore brands need level up their marketing game by sharing their storylines. It doesn't matter if you are just starting out or already have an established business. Just go ahead and share the real side of the business to strengthen the trust in your brand-customer relationships.

Transparency Tools for Social Media

It is important for brands to use transparency tools when it comes to social media marketing. Have you heard about the Facebook Transparency tool for the Ad campaigns?

There are some great tools that social media marketers use to improve the transparency of their ad campaigns on Facebook. How can you use the Facebook transparency tool for your brand's benefit, you ask? Let's learn how you can see advertisements of different Facebook pages and extract relevant data from them for your own use.

First, you need to go to your competitor's Facebook page to check their ads information. Once you are on the page, look at the left panel of the page and click on the "Info and Ads" tab. This action will redirect you to a new window where you will be able to see all the active ads of that particular page. It doesn't matter if you fall in their targeted audience or not.

Now it's time to use this transparency tool for your brand's growth.

1. Perform some research on your competitors

Using the transparency tool, you can find the advertisements of your competitors along with the content and visuals they have shared. Check on them thoroughly to see if they are offering anything unique, such as promotional deals.

Another important aspect to look at is the type of content they are using, whether its a static image or a video, the duration of the advertisement, along with the consumer market which they have selected to target. You need to read between the lines and understand the concept of that campaign from a marketer's point of view. See if the ad is focused on getting leads or redirecting them to a particular landing page. It's a great way to understand your competitor's mindset and create your social media marketing campaigns accordingly.

Note to remember: What works for your competitor doesn't ensure that it will work for your brand as well. Thus, it is important to develop your original content around your brand's personality while keeping in mind the key points from others' Facebook ads.

2. Keep an eye on new advertisement features of Facebook

Facebook has a thing for ad campaigns, and they make sure to roll out new features for the marketers that use the platform. It is great to adopt these new updates to see what's working and what's not. However, it does get difficult to identify the best use of such features. Brands work on allocated budgets per month, so a loss on trial and error wouldn't be a smart way to go about it.

That's when the ad transparency tool comes in play. It allows you to perform some pre-work before getting into the new ad features. The big brands are always seeking out brand-new ways to get ahead of others in terms of customer retention and satisfaction. Through the transparency tool, you can find out how other brands are using that new ad feature. This will allow you to understand the functionality of that new ad feature without investing a chime on your advertisements.

3. See what's trending

Facebook transparency tool also lets you to extract the type of products your competitors are selling out. You can see what's trending, what they are offering to the users, and what your brand can do to adopt the similar strategy. You can then strategize your content to enhance sales by offering product lines, which, of course, is relevant to your brand's personality.

Facebook Live - The Rising Trend

Facebook Live is a newly added feature on the platform that allows users to take real-time videos and show it to their followers. Different social media marketers are using this feature to increase audience engagement, sales, brand growth, and overall customer involvement.

These days, live videos are trending more than anything else. They are not only popular among large enterprises but are also for small organizations that want to target potential customers. While the concept of live video is becoming an effective tool for social media marketers, having a full grip of it can help brands utilize this tool in the right way.

To understand the marketing mechanism of Facebook Live, you need to understand its basic functionality. In truth, this feature gives you a chance to broadcast live videos on your business page or personal profile. It was originally released back in 2016. While many social media advertisers are wrapping their heads around this feature, the ones who are already using this feature are benefiting from it like a pro.

Once you take a video through Facebook Live, it stays there even after the broadcasting is over so that users can watch it later on your page or profile. After the algorithm change in Facebook, videos that are up real-time are shown on top instead of the pre-recorded ones. This creates an opportunity for the marketers to attract users toward a particular event, product promotion or a newsbreak.

Until now, you must have heard about the importance of video marketing and how it is making waves for brands across Facebook. According to a statistics, Live videos on Facebook receive three times more engagement than the recorded ones. Even for the standard images, the feature garners about five times more user engagement compared to videotaped versions.[9] Whether you want to create brand awareness, generate

---

[9] Kant, V. & Xu, J. (2016). Taking into account live video when ranking feed. Retrieved from https://newsroom.fb.com/news/2016/03/news-feed-fyi-taking-into-account-live-video-when-ranking-feed/

potential leads or increase audience engagement, therefore, Facebook live is your ultimate tool to pitch potential customers.

There are five proven Facebook Live techniques that you can use in your social media marketing campaigns:

1. It allows you to connect with your audience in the most genuine way possible

Do you ever want your followers to see your brand as a non-responsive platform? *Bet not.* Well, there isn't any other way to connect with your audience than doing a live session with them. Facebook Live gives you a medium to do a live broadcast and share your news, opinions, and thoughts with your potential audience. This strikes a sense of involvement for users and makes them feel more connected to your brand, hence the human interaction.

2. It answer their queries in real-time

If you want to do extra and be unique, then having a human connection with your followers is mandatory for successful marketing campaigns. Maintaining contact with your potential audiences doesn't need to be limited to when you check up on your brand's page. With Facebook Live, you can interact with them real-time by answering their queries and concerns through a live video session. This gives you a great opportunity to get your audiences used to your online presence.

Focus on your own industry and create recurring live sessions to keep your followers engaged in real-time. For example, if you sell beauty products, doing a live video chat to showcase different makeup items and answer some questions can help your customers learn more about your brand. Besides, it will make your followers feel acknowledged and would ensure customer satisfaction.

To hail this marketing strategy, you should stay consistent with your schedule when you plan to go on Facebook Live. It is ideal to have a field expert to lead the session as well or someone who can keep track of the queries in the comments sections.

3. It involves people on events that they cannot attend physically

Facebook Live is undoubtedly a great tool to involve customers in live broadcasts of events. It is especially beneficial for those who cannot attend it in person. This also allows you to connect with your followers around the world regardless of their location. Once you are live during an event, it is easy to virtually invite your subscribers. And as long as you have a fast-working internet connection and permission to use a live broadcast, you can benefit from it.

Pro tip: Make sure to take note of the comments on your live broadcast and answer them real-time. You might attract some potential leads for your business that way

4. It lets you share industry-based knowledge

If you want to retain your followers' interest in what you are offering, it is important to share other industry-based knowledge. This will keep them hooked and leave a positive impact on overall user engagement.

More Visuals, More Engagement

Visual content is one of the most powerful and growing trend on social media. Social media marketers are using visuals for brand growth and page engagement. Some of the most popular platforms that focus on visual content (e.g., infographics, images or videos) are Snapchat, Instagram, and Pinterest. Facebook, on the other hand, is a channel that uses a mix of visuals and text.

The way in which people – especially the young generation – are consuming the content is changing rapidly. There is no time for them to read long texts or go through dull content anymore. For a brand, therefore, it is important to grasp the attention of the users by showing them vibrant visuals with a short and crisp text that conveys the ultimate message.

You have one minute to attract the user's attention while they are searching for, sharing, downloading, shopping, and exploring the site. As a social media marketer, you need to increase the use of visuals in your content marketing strategy to stay consistent with the rapid demands and changes on different platforms.

What matters the most in your brand's strategy is customer satisfaction. If it is not your focus on your current plan, then you might need to revisit and revise your scheme. After all, you need to show your followers what they want to see while maintaining your brand's message. Visual content is a smart way of increasing user growth, brand awareness, lead generation, and sales. It also helps in enhancing the overall design of the brand on both the website and other social media platforms. As for Facebook, its algorithm keeps on changing and demands for rapid adoption. If you want to keep your posts on top of the newsfeed, then you will have to stick with a theme that resonates with your brand and correlates with what the users want.

There are a lot of visual content types to choose from, including: vibrant photos, illustrations, vector-based graphics, text-based visuals, one-word images, infographics, 360 live images, and short videos. With the ever-changing trends, these are excellent sources for social media marketers who wish to grasp users' attention and allow them to notice the content naturally.

Below are some visual statistics to look upon.[10]

- Approximately 80% of people only skim through the content they see online. This indicates that your brand needs to be vigilant in creating visuals that are eye-catching and attention-seeking even in a short timespan.

- The first impression of the brand is formed within half a second.

- About 84% of the user engagement done in 2018 was through visual content.

- In 2018, about 79% of the traffic was attracted by engaging short videos.

- Approximately 80% of the users are likely to buy your product after seeing a product-focused video. Videos are the next big thing in the marketing world; that's why you should extend your visual representation by showcasing your brand through interactive videos.

- Posts that consist of videos or video links generate three times more traffic engagement compared to text-based posts.

---

[10] Imgur. (2015). Humans are changing: How to adapt your brand [Infographic]. Retrieved from https://imgur.com/468Awwl

Chapter 2: Types of Facebook Ads

If you are among the one billion brands on Facebook, you might have noticed the changing trend when it comes to content. Video materials are taking over the newsfeed and proving to be one of the greatest content types of 2019.

As a social media marketer, you should understand the importance of videos for your brand. There are different types of video format available for brands. Each Facebook video ad type allow the businesses to showcase their best products. The marketing specialists on the platform are becoming aware of this rising trend, too, and trying to adopt various styles. As an entrepreneur, therefore, you want to focus on brand awareness and sales growth.

Previous statistics show that static images or text-based posts do not bring as much engagement as videos lately. In 2018, a research conducted by Adobe Digital Insights found that a lot of advertisers lose sales and audiences when they try the one-size-fits-all method in the United States.[11] There are diverse types of Facebook ads that you can adopt to run your campaigns as well. However, there is no definite rule that says that you should only use a single ad type. Brands can try different materials to see which one brings in the most engagement.

Nevertheless, everything drops down to the fact that you have to stand out among everyone. How can you compete with your competitors on Facebook advertisements while maintaining the quality standards and customers' interest? To accomplish this, you first need to understand different types of Facebook ads. Once you are well-versed with their importance, you can test them to engage with users on your page.

Showstopper - Video Ads

As discussed earlier, Facebook video ads are the top forms of advertisements that a brand can adopt. Videos are indeed a showstopper when it comes to user engagement and brand awareness. Instead of spending your time on writing short chunks of text or uploading a picture on your page, you can work on an engaging video either in-house or by hiring a professional videographer. Alternatively, you can upload your own native

[11] Adobe Digital Insights. (2018). State of digital advertising [Slideshow]. Retrieved from https://www.slideshare.net/adobe/adi-state-of-digital-advertising-2018

videos as long as they are of high quality. If you are filling your videos with useless content and fillers, then chances are that you will not get any views on it. The first 10 seconds of your video should convey the message of what users can expect to see later. Punch lines that attracts the customers' attention are going to work well on videos, too.

Consider the example of Nike's new ad - "Nike – Dream Crazier" - this year.[12] It lasted for only a minute and 30 seconds, but it managed to grasp the interest of viewers because of its title, content, as well as emotions conveyed through it. It was well-strategized as Nike released it with the message, "Show them what crazy dreams seem like." It positively provoked the feelings of viewers around the globe and became a perfect representation of an impactful video. Instead of focusing on your brand's great points, therefore, you should incorporate human emotions into your advertisements to create a sense of relatability.

Why Invest in Video Ads?

Video ads are the best form of Facebook advertisements as they ensure that people will remember your business. Visually appealing ads help you shine brighter than your competitors. They also work well for converting viewers into customers. Furthermore, ads provide enough data to marketers, which they can utilize on other platforms such as Instagram, Twitter, and LinkedIn.

Research shows that video content advertisements are going to stay for long and will allow brands to communicate with their audiences in a more interactive way.[13] A survey conducted by Hubspot earlier in 2019 also indicated that videos aren't just effective; instead, they are becoming a necessity for the brands. Some of the marketing facts and statistics to support the importance of video ads are shown below.[14]

- Approximately 54% of the population on social media platforms want to see video content rather than static images or text-based posts.

- The region that most demands for video content is Latin America.

---

[12] Nike. (2019). Nike - Dream Crazier [Video file]. Retrieved from https://www.youtube.com/watch?v=whpJ19RJ4JY

[13] Jones, B. (2016). In video advertising, Is longer stronger? Retrieved from https://www.thinkwithgoogle.com/consumer-insights/unskippable-video-advertising-ad-recall-brand-favorability/

[14] Kolowich, L. (2017). 16 video marketing statistics to inform your 2019 strategy [Infographic]. Retrieved from https://blog.hubspot.com/marketing/video-marketing-statistics

- Approximately 83% of the users across the web watch YouTube videos. This information indicates that clips available on any platform are going to attract more viewership and engagement than other visual types. Thus, it creates an opportunity for brands to share their content or story through videos and run ads using them to reach potentials users.

- There can be different video genres that can be adopted by brands. However, adopting to an entertaining type of videos generate more engagement. Around 73% of the population shows interest in "entertaining" videos as well, and so businesses should add elements of entertainment relevant to their products or services.

Before starting your own video-based campaigns on Facebook, you need to define a clear message that you want to convey through that visual type. You also have to decide about the ultimate objective of your advertisement. Say, do you want to send people from your video to a particular landing page, reach more potential clients within your locality, or something else? Nevertheless, when it comes to video ads, brands usually select "Get Video Views" with an aim to achieve potential leads from it.[15]

Workable Video Marketing Strategies to Increase User Engagement, Conversions, and Overall Play Rate

Videos with No Sound

This may sound absurd, but videos with no sound can actually attract consumers' attention. In this rapidly evolving social world, people don't have time to go through details and prefer to swipe through their newsfeed instead. Videos with sound may restrict them from open them, though, in certain scenarios.

To convey your message through a video without using sound, you can add subtitles to it. This will help viewers know what's going on in your video. Facebook recently shared a caption feature for advertisers considering the sound issue. Now, you may promote ads on mute. As a marketer or advertiser, it is important to invest in videos that sell while maintaining the factors of creativity and useful information.

Turn On Autoplay Feature

Would you want your Facebook video to get noticed? Users don't have the time to wait

---

[15] Facebook Business. (2015). The value of video for brands. Retrieved from https://en-gb.facebook.com/business/news/insights/the-value-of-video-for-brands

as they merely spend few seconds to see what a brand has to offer. If your video isn't on autoplay, chances are that you are going to lose potential views and clicks. So, if you want to engage those multitaskers, you need to ensure that your videos will play automatically. However, to become eligible to set videos on Autoplay, your brand has to bid for cost per impression (CPM) on Facebook. Cost per click (CPC) isn't going to help here because you need to get impressions, not clicks.

Keep It Short

Video ads are supposed to be short. Facebook allows a user to upload a two-hour long video, but who has the time to see an advertisement like that? If you want to gain attention, you need to focus on what they want to see and deliver it in the initial 45 seconds of the video.

In 2016, Wistia released data about how users engage with videos and how much time they spend on average. The data showed that, on average, around 80% of individuals watch videos that are shorter than 30 seconds. People lose interest if the video gets longer than that, and they usually drop out after 30 seconds.[16] If you want to stay in a safe zone, you can try to keep your video duration within the time limit of two minutes.

Fun Fact: Your 90-second video is going to leave the same impact as your 30-second video on the viewers. Just keep its duration under two minutes, and you are good to go.

Only Promote Videos That Performed Well on Other Platforms

To determine which videos performed well, you would have to ask yourself a few questions. For instance, which ones performed organically on your page? What kind of content was used in those videos that generated the most views? Which one among the live or recorded webinars gained most user engagement? It is important to realize the status of these core components - e.g., engagement, views, and shares of the previous videos - so that you can run similar video ads in the future. Investing money on them will help you gain more viewership, sales and user engagement.

Focus on Targeted Audience

Focused ads can bring potential leads and increase your sales. Instead of capitalizing on a video ad campaign that targets a vague and larger audience, it is better to granulize your target market and concentrate on people who are genuinely interested in the type of products or services you are offering. This way, you have great chances of receiving high engagement rate on your videos. This will also help in converting your viewers into

---

[16] Fishman, E. (2016). How long should your next video be? Retrieved from https://wistia.com/learn/marketing/optimal-video-length

potential customers. You can run ads using targeted audience, specific locations, demographics, interests, and behaviors of the users. Social media marketers can apply this strategy on different focus groups to see which ones bring in the best results.

Image-Based Advertisements

At first, Facebook advertising seems easy to set up and run. In reality, it's a bit tricky. Nevertheless, the more time you invest into planning your campaign, the more traffic it can bring to your content.

Although video ads got their place in the advertisement marathon, there is one great ad type that we cannot neglect when it comes to visually appealing content: image-based advertisements. The truth is that Facebook offered "picture advertisements" as one of its initial marketing tools. To bring the right traffic on your content, social media marketers need to adjust all the important aspects of it into one visually and aesthetically enticing image ad.

Image-based advertisements are one of the top ad types on Facebook. To successfully run this material, you should keep track of some of the technical requirements to ensure that the advertisement starts off with a bang. While the picture ads are the most basic ones, they are the most effective options as well. They are versatile in nature and can be used for any brand goal, e.g., brand awareness, sales or user engagement. Social Media Marketers can keep track of the following aspects:

- The image size should be no smaller than 1200 x 638 pixels. Any photo with dimensions lower than that will become distorted and may not be accepted by Facebook.

- Consider the platform's 20% rule. This means that you can only add 90 characters of text. If you will add too many words on the picture, Facebook may not run it even if you set a high budget. The site introduced this rule back in 2018, which has brought a lot restrictions for the advertisers. It has become important for brands to keep minimum text on the images to run them properly on Facebook.[17] This rule only applies on newsfeed advertisements, though, and not on right-panel advertisements.

Pro tip: Make sure to check your images on a 20% rule checker online to see where they stand in terms of text overlay. If every photo gets marks "OK," you are good to go.

---

[17] Vrountas, T. (2018). The Facebook 20% rule: Why your ads might not be running. Retrieved from https://instapage.com/blog/facebook-20-text-rule

Image ads are one of the great materials to showcase your products to potential customers and create awareness about them. Marketers need to understand that visually appealing pictures don't need to be difficult or expensive. A simple and elegant picture with an impactful text can bring in the right audience to your brand.

Image ads run directly in the newsfeed of the users. Brands get the ultimate chance to present their products to the world through a vibrant and impactful image. Marketers can use images of actual items in the ads to represent what the business is all about and what users can expect if they buy a particular product.

Another important aspect to keep in mind is the involvement of real humans into the ad. For instance, if you sell funky socks, you can either take an unappealing picture and post with a text or have models photographed while wearing those socks for your ad campaigns. Ads that show a familiar sense of social fabric for users generate more engagement and sales than those with only a product image.

Excessive text on ads can distract the audience and can result in less user engagement. Research shows that images with no to minimum text leave a more positive impact on consumers as compared to those cluttered with too much text. So, as a marketer, you need to keep track of this point for future image-based advertisements. The rule of thumb is to keep one message per image ad campaign. For example, if you are promoting a certain product or the upcoming launch of a new line, you have to make sure that each ad delivers a single message. It is vital to keep the ultimate goal in mind while downsizing the point of focus across your campaigns using different ad sets.

Furthermore, think about the visual consistency of the ad campaign. If you are running an ad campaign for a particular product, ensure that the color themes, font types, et cetera are consistent throughout the advertisement. Together, they will be able to deliver one message and help you run the brand's ads in a successful manner.

Users on Facebook prefer to see quality content, and that is where the marketers come in. It is your responsibility to use high-resolution images for the advertisements, for one. This will help you to promote ads on Facebook and adhere to the platform's quality standards at once.

Your brand doesn't have to hire a professional photographer to create appealing images. All you need to do is to pay attention to a few important aspects, such as the size and quality of the images that you plan to use in your advertisements.

Lastly, for the static picture ads marketers can experiment with different type of visuals to see what works best for a particular brand.

Collection Advertisements - E-Commerce Gateway

As discussed above, there are different Facebook ad types that brands can choose to promote their content with. However, some ads perform better than others, especially if you apply certain hacks and tricks. Talking about a great performing material, Facebook collection ads work like a charm if used correctly. This type of advertisement has a solid background of success stories. Considering you want your brand to be the next success story, you should incorporate collection ads into your brand's marketing strategies.

Collection ads were introduced back in 2017 and managed to grab the attention of advertisers due to their impressive performance, convenient design, and flexible customization options.[18] A usual collection ad includes either a video or an image followed by relevant product pictures. This ad type is great for brands that want to show several goods to the users without making the advertisement overwhelming for them.

One of the recent success stories showed that, during Christmas in 2018, Sephora ran a couple of ads using Facebook's collection ad format and received a 32% increase on their return on investment (ROI).[19] This is an example for all the brands out there that they can test and run a collection ad format for their own products and services.

When users click on your collection ads, they are redirected to a new window where a full image of the product gets displayed. Not only does it enhance the user engagement, but it also boosts sales. Most of the users prefer to scroll through their newsfeed using a mobile device; thus, it is important for marketers to optimize their ads accordingly. The great news is that collection ads work great on smartphones and tablets as they are specifically designed for mobile ads only and to maximize the experience of mobile users.

Facebook is now all about advertisement and how you use different tools to develop your brand awareness. They are best suited for users who are always looking for something new to look for. Customize your collection ads in a way that each one delivers the message of your ultimate campaign and ultimately converts your ad visitors into buyers.

Collection ads make a win-win situation for both marketers and Facebook as well,

---

[18] Peterson, T. (2017). Facebook's shoppable 'Collection' ad is its latest iAd-like format. Retrieved from https://marketingland.com/facebooks-shoppable-collection-ad-latest-iad-like-format-209886

[19] Facebook Business. (2018). Sephora. Retrieved from https://www.facebook.com/business/success/2-sephora

considering high-quality ads bring user engagement to the posts even from those individuals who are not very active on maintaining their profiles. There is a pool of people who do not use Facebook for connections. They keep it for shopping purposes since Facebook is becoming more of a business medium for both brands and individual consumers. A simple yet interactive video coupled with product images can attract the right audience and will increase the engagement rate on both the posts and the Facebook page.

Facebook collection ads are one of the core boosters for e-commerce market. If you run a brand that works in an e-commerce sector, and you still haven't added the collection ads in your marketing campaigns, then you are missing out on a lot of things. Collection ads are dynamic forms of advertisement that represent the actual brand identity along with products in front of potential users. You should invest into this particular ad type because collection ads help not only in selling goods but also in promoting your store with an extra flair and building your brand's image.

There are standard templates offered under the umbrella of collection ads, including: Instant Storefront, Instant Lookbook, Instant Storytelling, and Instant Customer Interest and Acquisition. These templates come in handy when creating interactive and vibrant advertising tools. Marketers always have the option to customize the ads as per brand owner's preferences and campaign objectives. Yo can see which ad sets are working and which aren't as well by trying different styles. The A/B testing provides a great platform to marketers to set different details for the same product.[20] The core components to keep in focus are:

- Headlines for each ad

- Offers proposed on both ads

- Copywriting done for each ad

- Visuals used on the main cover image of the advertisement

- Type and quality of product images used on both ad sets

All of these elements will help marketers see the performance of each ad and find out what factors influenced the sales through their campaigns.

---

[20] Karlson, K. (2019). Facebook ads A/B testing in 2019 – Why, what, and how to split test. Retrieved from https://karolakarlson.com/facebook-ad-ab-testing-rules/

Carousel Advertisements

Facebook carousel advertisements are among the most engaging and interactive ad types that brands can utilize to sell their products. Carousel ads are popular not merely because they are effective for the user engagement but also because of their layout options. After all, they provide a clean and concise medium to present the product line of a brand and allow a more interactive way of storytelling. These types of ads are a huge hit among e-commerce businesses as well. So, anyone who wants to sell their goods in a creative manner can invest into carousel advertisements.

Now, you will notice that most of the advertisers use the play cards to promote different aspects of one product. Social media marketers can use up to ten images to create a carousel ad. This means that you will have the leverage to promote ten different products under the umbrella of one ad. Carousel ads usually consist of ten cards, and each one can showcase what your brand has to offer. The latter has a separate description underneath every image, too, to explain the story behind that the product. This feature makes it super efficient for the brands as it allows the marketers to add different call-to-action buttons under each merchandise and lead to their specific landing pages. This is the amazing ad flexibility that you don't get with any other ad type. With the opportunity to use ten cards, you can target your potential prospects and let them know what you have to offer. One statistic indicates that carousel ads cost relatively less - approximately 30% to 50% in cost-per-conversions and approximately 20% to 30% in cost-per-click - as compared to a standard image-based advertisement.[21]

Carousel ads work best for the desktop placements. This ad type comes with a series of different cards; that's why businesses can demonstrate their story in a more elaborate way. Just because most users use mobile for internet browsing, though, the importance of desktop ads can be neglected by the brands already. A majority of Facebook users still prefer to use desktop when viewing their account on the platform.[22] You might not receive the same amount of user engagement as with collection ads, but using carousel ads can shed light to your brand and create an impactful image in users' mind and help you see an increase in the sales of promoted products.

There are other prominent perks of using carousel ads that brands can adopt for their own benefit and success as marketers can include them to their social media marketing

---

[21] Facebook Business. (n.d.). Carousel ads. Retrieved from https://www.facebook.com/business/ads/carousel-ad-format?ref=ens_rdr

[22] Enge, E. (2018). Mobile vs desktop usage in 2018: Mobile widens the gap. Retrieved from https://www.stonetemple.com/mobile-vs-desktop-usage-study/

strategy. One of the most important benefits that you can gain from carousel ads is the fact that it can be placed on both desktop and mobile. This option is not available for collection ads since they work on mobile placements only.

One advantage that carousel ads can also offer is the ease of ad customization and creation.[23] This gives the marketers an opportunity to make the advertisements more personal and drive traffic to specific landing pages through each carousel card. To evoke user interest in your products make, sure to play around with the designs, make interactive slideshows or use a mix of videos and pictures to portray your brand's message creatively. You can choose a total of four images (it can be one video that's supported by three images, for instance) in the main preview section. Make sure to use the top four contents in your preview ad, though, to attract users' attention for other carousel cards within the same advertisement.

Best Practices for Carousel Ads

Carousel ads are easy to set up and do not take much time to get customized and placed in comparison with collection ads. However, social media marketers can use some of the best practices below to make their ads look more creative and professional.

Always Use a CTA

The inclusion of CTAs can improve user engagement and click-through rate on your ads. If you are not getting audience, the budget that your brand has invested in the advertisement will practically go to waste.

Use Numerous Headlines

As a social media marketer it is your responsibility to test and try different headlines on each carousel card. This will help you understand which carousel card brought in the most traffic and which didn't. Then, on the basis of the results, you can use similar content and design type on future ads. This method can work well for various brands since you can highlight numerous offers or prominent features on each card.

Tell Your Brand's Story through a Series of Cards

If you are using enticing graphics and content in your carousel cards, then chances are that you will attract more traffic from people who want to learn more about your offers. It is indeed an amazing tactic to bring in the new potential customers to your landing pages either on Facebook or business website.

---

[23] Newberry, C. (2018). Social media advertising 101: How to get the most out of your budget. Retrieved from https://blog.hootsuite.com/social-media-advertising/

Instant Experience Advertisements

Considering the proliferation of Facebook advertisements and their types, there are still some unexplored techniques that marketers can use to boost sales and brand awareness. However, only few take the charge of exploring. So, if you want to stand out among your competitors, you should read along to learn about one of the unexplored gems of Facebook advertisements: Instant Experience.[24]

Exploration and usage of innovative techniques tend to perform well and bypass the generic ad perceptions and techniques that are blindly followed by the Facebook page admins or marketers. To understand the mechanism of what works on Facebook, marketers need to invest extra time to understand the changing Facebook algorithms and newsfeed. Once you get hold of what works through tried innovative techniques, you can start using those methods that bring your brand in the spotlight.

Instant Experience advertisements are one of those techniques that you must consider to bring an extra charm to your brand. Instant Experiment ads were formally known as "canvas ads" when they first rolled out. However, the name changed after a while based on different components, such as how instantly users reacted to the ads, what the reactions on the ads were, and so on.[25] Instant Experience ads enable a business to showcase a compelling brand history and story outside the confined walls of a regular feed. Facebook users can learn about the business by staying on its page and not getting redirected to external links, e.g., a website. This allows the social media advertiser to create an enthralling experience for the users by providing the type of content that they want to see. A comfortable browsing experience, after all, is one of the important aspects to look upon in Facebook advertisements, regardless of the ad type selected. Moving on, the platform encourages and promotes instant ads happily, considering the users don't get to leave Facebook.

Pro Hack: Facebook favors and appreciates instant experience advertisements over the regular traditional ones.

However, most social media marketers avoid using Instant Experience advertisements, which is a big loss for companies and leaves a lot of opportunities behind. The major reasons behind this decision are rooted to the fact that these ads require more time and

[24] Weaver, B. (2018). Facebook Instant Experience ads: The new and improved canvas ads. Retrieved from https://instapage.com/blog/instant-experience-ads

[25] Page, M. (2018). How to create a Facebook Instant Experience ad (previously canvas ads). Retrieved from https://thedigiterati.com/how-to-create-a-facebook-canvas-ad-now-known-as-instant-experiences/

attention to details than traditional ads, they seem more complicated in terms of settings and customization, and they require more creativity to hook the right audience. If you are among those brands, then you should reconsider utilizing this form of advertisement. Instant Experience ads are the breakthrough type of advertisement that can genuinely introduce a lot of potential clients to your products. So, if you want to take advantage of this amazing Facebook ad type, then invest in your time in creating visually appealing designs and support them with relatable headlines. Even if you don't have pro designing skills, you can always use pre-made Facebook templates, which have been designed specifically for Instant Experience ads.

See some of the major advantages of using this marketing tool below.

- They are light-weighted ads and load instantly.

- They are properly optimized for the mobile users and perform well on the same medium.

- They are designed and formatted in a way that attracts the attention of the users, especially the targeted audience, and that is beneficial to the brand.

- It allow consumers to interact with brands, engage in interactive conversations, swipe through images and videos, as well as pan and tilt the advertisements to explore new products.

- It provides pre-made versatile Facebook ad templates that marketers without professional designing abilities can use.

- Instant Experience Ads can be expanded on a full screen to improve users' buying experience.

- They are designed to work on all formats, including static images, videos, graphics, slideshows, carousel, and even on collection ads.

Brands can utilize this innovative approach towards advertising to ensure user involvement and brand awareness. It's a great way to showcase what a brand has to offer to potential and existing customers. As a marketer, you will need some time to adopt the working mechanism of Instant Experience ads. However, once you get accustomed to it, you can definitely see the obvious changes that it will bring to the table. To start successfully, make sure to use your own premium product images along with unique content to be able to compete against the mainstream ads on Facebook. Make sure to use a simple and easy-to-follow pathway for the users as well using CTAs, texts, links, and buttons that can enhance users' buying experience.

Facebook is a great platform when it comes to promoting your products and services.

Overtime, it has developed into a great medium for both brands and customers. Considering the amazing details that Instant Experience advertisements provide, marketers now have more control over what they want to show and sell to their users. Similarly, from the users' perspective, they can explore different buying options at a single space and invest their money on the desired products or services that they appreciate. Even if you are only starting as a new brand, investing into instant ads can boost your brand's presence and create a positive image for your goods. You don't have to set aside a large amount of dollars these ads; use a limited budget that suits your brand and keep your focus on the quality of graphics and headlines.

Chapter 3: Marketing on Instagram

Instagram is a great platform for marketing. In the eight years that passed by since it's official launch, the platform paved a way for itself like a storm through the digital space. Instagram has evolved over the years and now offers great features that users can play with anytime. Social media marketers and influencers are the ones who are benefiting the most from this innovation.

Have you ever thought about the importance of Instagram for your brand, though? Have you ever wondered if the image-sharing platform is a good fit for your business marketing strategy? Below are some of the recent statistics that might be able to help you figure out whether you should bring your business to Instagram or not.[26]

- Instagram has more than 800 million monthly users, which equates to a massive potential market that brands can target for specific products and services.

- Among this population, approximately 60% of adults use an Instagram app for connections, business engagement, and product purchases.

- Instagram currently has more than 25 million active business page handles.

- About half of the users on Instagram follow at least one business page/brand.

- 60% of the population expressed that they learned about a brand's particular product or service through the platform.

It is quite evident that Instagram is not used for personal use alone. The available business opportunities on the channel has allowed different brands to come forward with their stories. It has turned into a global platform for businesses, influencers, digital nomads, and even growth hackers. Social media marketers now have the means to humanize their unique content, showcase present or upcoming products, hire new talent, and eventually inspire their followers through Instagram.

The great thing about Instagram is that it allows users to engage with brands. If you still haven't convinced about the significance of Instagram app, then here is another information for you: approximately 36% users visit the Instagram app multiple times within a single day.[27] This indicates that brands have a lot of potential to create

---

[26] Collins, A. (n.d.). Instagram marketing: The ultimate guide. Retrieved from https://www.hubspot.com/instagram-marketing

[27] West, C. (n.d.). Retrieved from https://sproutsocial.com/insights/new-social-media-

awareness and hook audience for long-term engagement. Instagram allow users, may it be individuals or brands. to promote their products or services using different marketing tools and options without adopting the standard cold-calling culture and by using vibrant and friendly marketing tactics instead.

Use of Hack Culture

Instagram is a trending app that works as a great platform for businesses. Most entrepreneurs develop an interest to create a brand and emerge as a successful one without any major efforts because of it. They share content that captivates followers' attention and makes it the talk of the town for days or weeks. However, the question, is how is it possible for any brand, especially a new one, to have a boosted start like this? How do they achieve such rapid growth and user engagement in the initial stage? How do these businesses sustain their online presence for months on Instagram despite the high competition that they face every day?

There is a very basic yet an impactful strategy behind it. It is commonly referred to as 'growth hacking". It is the newest technique that brands are adopting to stay ahead of their game. Brands invest in recruiting growth hackers to work on available marketing options and figure out how they can infuse different advertising strategies to obtain rapid and instant response. Efficient social media marketers on Instagram perform various experiments while keeping the marketing funnel in mind, which includes: sales, user engagement, product development, product placement, and other important elements. This helps them to formalize a workable marketing strategy for their brands on Instagram.

How can you use growth-hacking techniques to boost your brand's image and sales? Before jumping into the working advertising strategies mentioned above, you first need to keep note of the following advice.

- Once your thinking process focuses on growth hacking, you cannot back off anymore. Your brand needs to stay consistent with the newest digital tricks and practices to be able to surpass its competitors.

- You need to be ultra-efficient in creating your strategy because it will be a shame to waste money and effort on a campaign that may not work.

---

demographics/#Instagram

- You cannot enter your targeted niche market with an assumption that you will rank on top of all search engines or even on Instagram. You have to understand how ranking works on such platforms to gain a realistic view of things.

Growth hacking is not about investing hundreds of dollars for marketing. Instead, as a social media marketer, you are supposed to experiment with different content types and several inexpensive workable strategies. To use Instagram as a professional marketing personnel, you will have to beat the existing trends and advertising techniques, which others may already be using. That will allow you to come up with ingenious and innovative ways to meet your targeted goals. Before getting started with the growth hacking process, though, you also need to find the answer to the following questions within yourself.

- What do you need Instagram for? Is it for personal or product branding?

- What does growth mean to you or your brand? Do you want to create a brand image or increase user engagement?

- Do you have any specific time period in mind to achieve that goal? Have you set any parameters?

- To what extent can you invest into new experiments? What is the ideal marketing budget for you?

- How do you plan to use new growth-hacking ideas on your old techniques to improve the final outcome?

Get started with proven growth-hacking strategies once you have everything on board and are clear about your goals. The breakdown of the growth-hacking strategies are explained below.

Experiment with Numbers

People prefer quality content over quantity - that's a fact that applies to any situation. However, when it comes to growth hacking, your ultimate strength lies in the numbers.

Dropbox is a great example to look at. Their goal was to increase signups and the number of users on their platform. To achieve this, the company incentivized their current users to bring in more people on board. What was in it for the existing customers, you ask? Well, Dropbox offered a free storage space of up to 32GB, and they get 1GB after each referral. It was a great growth-hacking trick that the brand thought of doing to reach their potential customers in minimum time.

Do you think that Dropbox had to allocate extra budget for this marketing campaign? Most likely. When you are focused on achieving brand growth, though, such secondary aspects do not matter because, in the end, it all drop downs on growing the number of users on your brand's page. Considering the importance of numbers, increasing your followers on Instagram should be your prime objective. After all, growth hacking needs a blitz influence. You need people talking about your campaign.

Social media marketers can incorporate the same strategy that Dropbox used for their specific brands or products. This technique will create a beneficial relationship for both brands and users. After you build a sustained momentum through the marketing campaign, it will enable you to engage users for future posts.

Another aspect to take into consideration is "scaling." You can scale your growth rate during the marketing campaign to realize what your Instagram followers want to see and what triggers their genuine interest in your brand. Furthermore, to retarget your audience group, you should create a viral effect using your existing user engagement and reach. To achieve this, the "more is more" approach is ideal.

How do you gain the right followers for your Instagram page? To begin with, you can take into consideration the following points.

1. Follow the followers of the brands related to your field

If a user follows an Instagram account of someone else with the same interests as you do, then chances are that they are likely to follow you as well. This hack is ideal for getting potential targeted users without having to do any extra legwork.

How can you attract followers to your brand? Put in your brand-focused hashtag in the search bar. Say, for this specific guide, we can use #socialmediamarketing. Choose the hashtag that appears on the top of the dropdown menu. This will enable you to see top Instagram posts related to this particular hashtag. Select any top three posts and see who's behind it. (For example, is it an individual influencer or an established brand?) Check out the list of their followers as well and follow the ones whom you think would be best suited for your business goals You will have more chances to get followed back through this growth-hacking strategy.

2. Go on a commenting and heart-liking spree

This is a great approach to target potential users. Type in your brand-relevant hashtag in Instagram's search bar. Look for some promising accounts, review their content, like a few posts there, and leave thoughtful comments to strike a conversation. This will enable your brand to get the right user engagement and fan following. Make sure to interact with three different accounts on daily basis.

3. Post daily during the prime hours

Quality content is crucial for a brand's success. If you are not posting new content on daily basis, you are going to lose current followers and won't attract any new one either. Like any other social media platform, Instagram has optimal times for posting. You can analyze the data from your current posts to see which posts performed well. Keep track of the time and specific hours when they peaked, too.

As a pro tip, you should post content on off-hours and during peak hours. The best time to post images on Instagram is between 8 A.M. to 9 A.M. Videos, on the other hand, should be posted around 9 o'clock in the evening. Statistics show that videos posted around this time gets 34% more user engagement compared to other timings.[28]

4. Use niche-specific hashtags

Industry-focused hashtags work like a charm for any business or entrepreneur. Hashtags for Instagram ar no different from keywords that people use in search engines. Users type hashtags to find content on the platform; that's why you should make sure to utilize them a lot.

However, there is a limit to hashtag use by Instagram. A single post can merely have 30 hashtags at max. It is not recommended to stuff your post with unnecessary hashtags either because that might make viewers think that you did not brainstorm enough. Instead, it is best to maintain a balanced hashtag-to-content ratio in your posts. Too many irrelevant hashtags can reduce fan following and affects user interactions.

These are some of the strategies that you can use to increase the number of your followers on Instagram. As you put together your growth hacking marketing campaigns, it will enable you to grow your subscribers on the platform organically.

Create Lifestyle-Specific Narrative Content for Your Audience

Remember that short-term growth does not bring long-term results. Many brands make the mistake of investing into growth-hacking campaigns that only last for awhile and then frizzle out eventually. Nevertheless, have you ever wondered why they burn out instead of having impactful and lasting impression?

The reason is that they do not put their focus on sustainability. Instagram is all about

[28] Mawhinney, J. (2019). 45 visual content marketing statistics you should know in 2019. Retrieved from https://blog.hubspot.com/marketing/visual-content-marketing-strategy

quality content and user engagement. If your strategy does not include long-term growth-hacking techniques for user sustainability, then you are in trouble. You will be able to sustain the success of your brand by putting forward a lifestyle-specific narrative content for the audience. This idea involves the following practices.

- Create something scalable that you can sell to your audience through daily posts.

- Deliver a memorable experience for your followers. This won't cost you anything. All you need to do is show your brand's story in a creative manner.

- Invest on building a brand image that can advertise for itself even with minimum efforts coming from you.

- Brainstorm for ideas that makes you unique. Set that unique culture for your brand so that your competitors can't compete, reverse engineer or replicate your scheme.

Era of Instagram Stories

Instagram stands apart from all other social media platforms when it comes to creativity and innovation. Every new feature launched by the channel brings in a lot of fresh opportunities for the business-minded folks. It is one of the best platforms to sell your products or services in front for the right audience. Instagram has grown by 1400% over the past few years.[29] With this amazing change, it is a no-brainer for all the social media marketers to incorporate the social networking site into their marketing strategies.

Instagram Stories is another great feature introduced to users that want to showcase their brand. These stories make it easy for social media marketers to interact with other sellers, humanize connections, improve sales, create leads, and generate more consumers on this interactive platform. Instagram stories are a great marketing tool for showing your existing and potential clients why your brand is different from others yet relatable to them. So, if you are still struggling about whether to use Instagram stories for marketing purposes or not, now is the time to make a decision.

Using Instagram Stories for Your Brand

Creating an interactive Instagram story is pretty easy. However, Instagram has released a lot of new features within Instagram Stories, which have made it bit challenging to

[29] Patel, N. (n.d.). The marketer's guide to Instagram Stories: Building Your brand and generating sales [Blog Post]. Retrieved from https://neilpatel.com/blog/marketers-guide-to-instagram-stories/

keep track of all of your activities. We'll get back to these changes later on, but for a starter, let's see how you can create Instagram stories and use them for your brand's success.

- You can open your Instagram profile and upload a video by clicking on the camera icon on the top-left screen of the app.

- Users can record videos by pressing down the record button. Usually, ten-second videos work well on Instagram. Brands can use various video ideas as well to showcase their services or products. E.g., live, type (using preloaded fonts), normal, superzoom, boomerang, focus, rewind, and hands-free video.

- Brands can also use product images in stories along with in-built stickers and call-to-action buttons.

These points are just the basic things that brand owners should keep in mind. To stand out in the crowd of entrepreneurs, you need to have a separate content marketing strategy for Instagram Stories. An increase in user engagement, page growth, sales, and views may take place once you have a game-changing plan. To achieve this goal, marketers can use a mix of fun and creative content that must give positive vibes to the audience.

When making a strategy for Instagram Stories, you should remember that everything you create, post, and share must align with your brand goals. How do you create content that appeals your audience attention, you ask? You can do it by analyzing the data from the previous posts. Business profiles have the option to see insights for each post at the backend. This enables them to pinpoint key takeaway points, such as audience's age range, number of views and impressions, interactions, top locations, gender, and followers' increase rate. All these elements allow you to strategize a more interactive marketing strategy for the followers.

Here is a refresher on how you can incorporate different Instagram Stories' features to boost your brand discoverability. If you are sponsoring your Instagram stories for a particular product promotion, then you need to add in the best features to make it stand out among competition. Below are a few things that you can do to enhance your promoted Instagram Stories.

- Turn on your location. This will help you target potential customers within your locality. This feature will also make your page discoverable to all the users.

- Make use of relevant hashtags in your Instagram Stories. People use different hashtags in the Explore section to find relevant content.

These features have played a major role for the success of many brands. Whereas entrepreneurs could initially share their Instagram stories only with their own followers, now they are discoverable by anyone across Instagram since people can explore them by typing specific locations and hashtags. That's why it is recommended to use brand-specific hashtags and locations on your Instagram Stories. If you attract enough user engagement, you might end up appearing in the Explore section of Instagram.

Embed Links in Instagram Stories

If you have more than 8,000 followers on your Instagram account, then getting a straight-up traffic for your website won't be an issue. With Instagram Stories, though, you can redirect users to particular products pages within Instagram and in your site. This offers a great opportunity for businesses that want to increase brand engagement and product sales. Instagram users swipe up the screen of the stories and get redirected to specific URLs. It goes with saying that using Instagram Stories to redirect potential users to your product pages will eventually generate more leads.

Tag Other Accounts with Same Interests to Boost Brand Engagement

Instagram Stories is an effective medium to run contests on the platform as well. Such competitions are ideal for bringing user engagement and new followers to the page. Tagging other accounts into your Instagram Stories is a great way to build audience interactions. It is also great for affiliate marketing, considering you can market an individual, a design or a product by posting a particular story. This will help your brand gain more followers from other accounts. Be sure to share content that aligns with your business goals by tagging accounts with same interests as your brand.

Invest in Buying Ads for Content Distribution

Buying ads can play a vital role in every brand's content distribution plan. Businesses invest into the promotion and advertising of content to create brand awareness. To run sponsored posts, you will need to allocate a monthly budget. However, monthly budgets for Instagram marketing campaigns depend on numerous factors and vary from one business to another. The platform is pretty heavy on the visuals as well; thus, text ads won't work well here. If you want your marketing strategy to succeed on Instagram, you may rely on a single image, a collection of images or a video.

As a startup brand, you might question yourself as to whether you need to invest in Instagram marketing or not. The answer entirely depends on your business goals. If you are on Instagram to engage more followers, for instance, then organic posts may not function greatly for you. To build an audience base, you will have to put forward the creative side of your brand. As mentioned above, Instagram audiences prefer to see visuals that are appealing, informative and valuable in their lives. However, you might not be able to reach your potential customers through natural methods of waiting for people to come across it and hoping that others will talk about it online since Instagram has changed its algorithm and now prioritize sponsored posts over organic ones.

Is Instagram the right platform for your business? Does it have the audience group that you plan to target? You first need to ask these questions, too. If you are looking to target older population on Instagram, for example, then your chances of increasing your brand awareness and sales are low. Instagram is more useful to youngsters than anyone, frankly speaking. Almost 55% of the population on Instagram consists of young people aged between 18 and 29.[30]

Just like Facebook, Instagram provides vast advertising options to businesses and gives you the ultimate control to target focused audiences, age groups, demographics, gender, interests, and locations. Once you have the right content on hand, you can distribute it to your targeted audience through paid promotions and advertisements. The costs of advertisements depend on numerous factors and, unfortunately, most of these factors are not accessible for general users. The silver lining is that most ad results are based on cost per click (CPC) and cost per impression (CPM), and businesses are charged for their advertisements on Instagram's ad auction.

Influencer Marketing - Sponsored Content

In today's digitally evolving world, there is a strong competition between businesses to entice focused audience towards their brands by converting them into long-term loyal consumers. Brands on Instagram are now collaborating with different industry-relevant influencers to bring new customers and increase their brand's return on investments.

Brands are now interested in attracting audience that are potential for their brand. To do so, they are now teaming up with micro, macro, and mega influencers. It's a financial challenge for brands to hire celebrities for their promotion, thus, they are more interested in investing their budget into influencers with huge fan followings on Instagram. They are the real deal on the platform, after all. They play authentic and form a bridge between brands and focused audience.

Influencer marketing on Instagram is becoming a solid part of Instagram. It is also gaining popularity as a potential strategy that increases brand image and user engagement. A recent study conducted by Linqia highlighted that, in 2017, approximately 76% of the social media marketers used influencer marketing for the

---

[30] da Chunha, M. (2019). The complete guide to advertising on Instagram. Retrieved from https://www.wordstream.com/blog/ws/2017/11/20/instagram-advertising

promotion of their brands.[31]

Brands can leverage their sales and brand awareness by taking influencers on board. Apart from boosting brand image, influencer marketing helps in attracting potential leads and conversions. Influencer marketing is great for businesses; however, most marketers fail to incorporate it properly in their marketing strategies. To get the most out of influencer marketing, it is important for marketers to have a well-defined marketing strategy.

How to Create a Strong Partnership with Brands

So, how can you involve influencers into your brand's marketing plan? This can be achieved by following a series of steps. These steps include defining your business goals and connecting them with the right influencers for scalable growth.

Set Brand Specific Objectives

The influencer you will select for your brand and the content you generate will be dependent on the final result that you aim to attain. Hence, it is vital to have clear objectives at the start of the marketing campaign.

Do you want influencer marketing to increase sales? Do you want to promote a particular product or increase your return on investment? Having a defined objective makes it easier for influencers to showcase your content in the right way. It will also enable you to lay a solid foundation for your influencer marketing and advertising strategy.

Choose Suitable Influencers for Your Brand's Promotion

The influencer that you will hire for your brand's promotion should bring a huge impact on your overall marketing campaign. The first thing that you need to ensure is that the influencer must be from the same industry or niche as your own brand. This guarantees that your product or service will be shown to the audience with same interests. Furthermore, you need to ensure that the overall tone and content of the chosen influencer aligns with your brand's tone. Lastly, keep track of your sponsored content on the influencer's profile. See how the post is performing in terms of engagement, views, and impressions.

3. Use Quality Content

---

[31] Linqia. (2017). The value of influencer content 2017 [PDF File]. Retrieved from http://www.linqia.com/wp-content/uploads/2017/04/The-Value-of-Influencer-Content-2017_Final_Report.pdf

The quality of content should remain your first priority. The use of influencer marketing for promotion of posts is not an exception here. Brands must maintain the standards of quality content so that your promotion won't leave any scalable impressions. Even if you collaborated with the top influencer, you need to ensure that it provides the highest quality. You can make sure of that by infusing interesting and informative content into one. It is also recommended to discuss content ideas with influencers as they can guide you better with what works on Instagram.

IGTV - The Next Arising Trend

Things are certainly changing for Instagram. IGTV is all set to redefine the meaning of branding. IGTV is Instagram's exclusive platform that allow brands to showcase their services and products in a creative manner. It was launched back in June 2018 and has paved its way towards rapid growth ever since. It allow users to upload a ten-minute long video, which you can share on your account. For all the verified profiles, businesses can upload a 60-minute long video.[32]

By 2021, about 78% of the population will shift to mobile devices.[33] IGTV was introduced on the foundation of these statistics, considering more people are now turning to digital videos. It is a great feature for brands to connect with their audience and be discovered by new users on Instagram. IGTV is somewhat similar to YouTube, in the sense that entrepreneurs can make channels on the medium and publish content on daily basis. However, IGTV did not receive that much hype even after the first six months of the launch. Most industry experts doubted that this feature might fall out by the start of 2019. Surprisingly, IGTV downloads started to increase in number at the end of 2018 and are still rising in 2019. This proves that the doubts indicated by some of the online specialists were premature. Just like any other digital feature, IGTV finally began to get the hype it deserved. Currently, one out of four brands are investing their time in creating content for IGTV channel. This indicates possible opportunities for brands who still haven't tried their luck in the medium.

Pro Tip: Small businesses can use IGTV to raise brand awareness and user engagement,

---

[32] Phelan, D. (2018). Why IGTV is Instagram's bravest update yet: Longer video app to take on YouTube (Updated). Retrieved from https://www.forbes.com/sites/davidphelan/2018/06/21/instagram-reveals-igtv-dedicated-hub-and-new-app-for-much-longer-videos/

[33] Doeing, D. (2018). 58 powerful video marketing statistics for 2019. Retrieved from https://learn.g2crowd.com/video-marketing-statistics

considering only few brands are currently investing into it.

Chapter 4: Building Audience

Building an audience for your brand is not that difficult in today's fast-moving digital world because we have endless digital marketing options available on all the social media platforms, including Facebook and Instagram.

Firstly, we all know that Instagram is owned by Facebook. You can build an audience on these channels both organically and with paid advertising. The two platforms have gotten most popularity for advertising in recent years among other social networking sites. As a social media marketer, you need to understand a few key points to build up a solid audience base on your pages in the future. Read along and learn more about the tactics of creating different segments of audience.

Nowadays, It's All About VISUALS!

Nurture your potential clients with an excellent visual-driven experience using social media that will lead to engaging and loyal audience. After all, we believe in what we see, such as Feedback and brand collaboration with top bloggers and paid and organic social media.

According to a recent study, approximately 86% of the digital marketers use these two (paid and organic) tactics in their social media marketing and content strategies. Everyone all around the world are advertising ads on both platforms altogether to reach more potential users.[34]

You can run ad campaigns on both channels at the same time by clicking the checkbox under the ad set's placement portion on Facebook, which connects it to your Instagram account. It increases traffic on your website, as well as customer views, clicks, and engagements simultaneously. Organic social media is used to develop your brand name. Additionally, paid campaigns may allow you to accelerate audience growth and boost revenue. To accomplish this for your brand, you can create ads that can run on both platforms. Distribute your content with paid ads and organic postings, and then choose the best targeting options. Maximize your brand personality through strategic paid promotions using user-oriented content, too. This is what develops a connection between a brand and its customers.

---

[34] Finn, A. (2018). Facebook Ads Manager vs Power Editor: Which is better?. Retrieved from https://www.wordstream.com/blog/ws/2017/08/22/facebook-ads-manager-vs-power-editor

Content, Content, and Content

Yes, this era is all about content, content and content! How? Let's talk about it below.

Content marketing has become a necessity of every brand as it is useful for their promotions and distinctive brand image among other competitors. In order to present the audience with the right marketing paraphernalia, you need to plan how you want to create a brand image. Say, what strategies are you currently applying, and which other possible options do you have? What is your audience type? What kind of high-quality content do you plan to present in front of thousands of potential users? The essence of content marketing is to provide interesting and valuable information to the audience. Social media advertisers who work for different brands use Facebook and Instagram as base platforms for audience growth.

Informative and Useful Content

How you present your brand's story or message on a social media platform plays a vital role in any content management strategy. We are living in a digitally evolving world; hence, adapting to rapidly changing social media trends is what you should do for your brand. Social media never sleeps; it's always online and connected. What matters is how you use the platforms within your reach to attract the right audience, may it be through solid content strategy or visually appealing infographics or banners.

Content Calendar

A recent study suggests that 78% of consumers buying intention increases if relevant content is provided on their social platform.[35] So, smart marketers who understands this need invest more time in creating content calendars, to organize and plan-out content for the whole month.

Relevant Content Marketing Plan

To engage and delight the audience, social media marketers work on the true image of their brand coupled with a strategic plan that answers every query of the customer. For instance, what is the actual story behind the brand? What type of products and services a brand offers?

Data-Driven Content

---

[35] Launchway Media. (2018). 16 statistics that prove personalized content works [Blog Post]. Retrieved from https://www.launchwaymedia.com/blog/2018/5/14/16-statistics-that-prove-personalized-content-works

Everything that shines on social media is not true, and it becomes difficult for brands to gain user's trust. However, how you present the information matters. In order to stand out among the sea of competitors, to be specific, your brand needs to adopt the transparency factor, show factual stats, and avoid spreading incomplete and fake information. High-quality content such as industry articles, videos, infographics, podcasts, and other materials can be used with all the necessary information to form a relationship of trust with a large number of audience. Brands can also attract the target audience by showing the content that matters to them and to the business.

Understand the Audience's Preferences

Understanding users' preferences is the most significant aspect of audience building.

As a social media marketer, you need to be prepared with a plan or strategy that covers the demands of the consumers for your brand through your content. Half of the milestone is already achieved if you know what it means.

Quality Over Quantity Through Content Marketing

You should be posting short, original videos and vibrant images to captivate the attention of the audience. Leave a concise and impactful message in any of them because people spend only few seconds on the content. If you fail to convey your message instantly, the audience will lose interest and potentially reduce engagement to your page.

Building Brand Trust

Reputation building between you and your audience through great content is very important. It is vital for brands to work towards creating a trust level with their customers because it will establish a positive brand reputation afterward.

Brands Should Showcase Their Subject Matter

The integral part of building trust and developing a positive brand reputation can only be done if you show your audience what your business does. In a recent research, it was demonstrated that brands that share their actual information and expertise are liked by the huge group of the users because this enhances their buyer journey and overall user experience.[36]

---

[36] Wallace, T. (n.d.). [Infographic] Modern consumer behavior in the new omni-channel world + 31 expert tips to dominate it now. Retrieved from https://www.bigcommerce.com/blog/consumer-behavior-infographic/#31-experts-on-

Keeping Future Content Marketing Trends in Mind

Initially, it may seem hard to align content marketing with social media advertising for future trends. However, once you study about the available possibilities of each trend, it becomes a lot easier to understand things like brand goals, objectives, buyer's personas, product placement, et cetera.

Content Is Advertising

No matter what you read on the internet, content is always a form of advertisement for your brand. Focus on making a strategy that positively entices people to seek out your products and services in the future.

Considering Getting the Help of SEO

You must be wondering how search engine optimization (SEO) helps here. Through research and data gathering, you came to know what a customer searches for in a specific store online. Now, writing blogs and articles related to that variable will let the consumers find valuable content on your website if they are only typing a general concern or question into a "search engine" box.

Influencers Love Content

Make influencers fall in love with your brand's content marketing strategy. There is a famous trend that has started, which says that influencer marketing is the new content king. Do you know why?

The reason is that influencer marketing is like working in collaboration with a renowned person on either Instagram or Facebook in a specific niche to distribute content that encourages an online audience to take a course of action. E.g., make a purchase from your brand after watching a promoted video or content or visit the website. Content marketing is all about creating the perfect material to attract potential customers from the market, and brands can employ the help of influencers to promote their name or products in general. Influencer marketing involves taking the perfect content and finding the best individual to advertise it.

---

dominating-an-omnichannel-strategy

Create Audience Segments

Audience segmentation is a very important tool in a marketer's world. When you divide audiences into different segments based on their needs, then you are going to get more leads from your social media platforms.[37]

Here, a question arises! Why it is so important to split up your target market?

Before taking your first step, you must develop your knowledge about the audience engaged with your brand on Facebook, Instagram, and other social media channels. Getting the information about your typical customers and how they engage with your posts such accounts will help your business grow in a more productive way.

Basically, the main purpose of audience segmentation is to find ideal clients for your business. If you keep this in mind - right target market leads you to the right audience - the money that you have invested into your business may return to you in heaps.

When we say the word "audience segmentation," it means it is divided into further portions.

First Type - Demographics: Age, gender, occupation, size of family and education.

Second Type - Psychographics: Attitude, social class, and their lifestyle.

Third Type - Behavioral: Users' online presence and website usage.

Fourth Type - Geographical: Country, city, and area.

Every business is based on these four types, depending upon their strategy and how they implement it.

Targeting Audience Segmentation
There are three types of audience's you can target:

Saved Audiences

This part allows you to target a specific segment of the audience, which includes their interests, location, income level, behaviors, and other specifications.

Custom Audiences

---

[37] Harrison, K. (n.d.). Audience segmentation is important for better communication [Blog Post]. Retrieved from https://cuttingedgepr.com/free-articles/core-pr-skills/audience-segmentation-important-better-communication/

This area includes an audience that is already familiar with your business and is added in your customer list. The data about them can be gathered through website visits or engagement with your content.

Lookalike Audiences

Engaging with custom audiences will lead you towards a lookalike audience as the former type contains a target market that has no previous interaction with your business. When you say "lookalike," it refers to new people who share the same characteristics as your source audience.

How else we can segment our social media audience? When it comes to fragmentation, you can find out more about life events and purchasing behaviors of the audience.

Purchasing Behavior

By combining the loyal purchasing records and profile data of the consumer, you can segment your audience according to the things they purchase and how often they do it.

Life Events

It involves sentiments. You must know whether a consumer's purchasing decision and the brand's sentiments are related to a major life event, such as birthdays, wedding parties, and holidays.

Test and Learn Different Content

Good content is the major key to success for any brand's hard work and effort on social media. Now, you need to not only create that content but also promote it on your accounts on various platforms. Creating quality material alone will not help you increase the number of followers on your page, though. If you want to reach potential users, you will have to boost posts using paid promotions.

Sometimes you come across a great piece of content. You might have read it online through blogs, articles, email, infographic or book. No matter where you came to learn about that information, it is a good example of content promotion. Most of them appear on your newsfeed as well, and they are either sponsored or promoted through those brands. In case you are wondering why you see them, the reason is that you fall under the targeted audience of that particular advertisement.

Basics to Writing an Affirmative Content

To craft the perfect blog post, you have to work through these steps: research background properly, optimize content, use targeted keywords to rank for, and use relevant links along with creative images and infographics. Via focused content strategy, you can develop an engaging blog post for your website and reshare it on Facebook and Instagram to gain more views.

Unique Content Creation Is Incredibly Important

When we have limited resources, creating a unique content and promoting it on social media channels can be a big challenge. Nevertheless, it is well-worth the hard work. In a competitive market, using different forms of content will play a huge role to get you on the top of the list because being unique is a new trend. People respond to fresh and creative ideas more instantly. To try test and learn different content types, you need to work on the following steps:

Research Thoroughly

You need to look at your industry competitors at this point because marketing trends and techniques are always changing. Conducting an extensive research before developing a new content is very important. As you look at the market, you will get new ideas and create something that has not been offered in your area before. You can adopt those ideas and implement them in your brand's strategies. This way, you will be able to work on the creation of unique content.

Track All Your Efforts and Results

You can check you strategy's progress through this process:

Content promotion is the key to focus on!

Divide it into three weeks and check its progression.

Week 1:

Facebook: Post five times per day at peak times.

Instagram: Post one time per day at peak Instagram time.

Week 2:

Facebook: Post four times per day at peak times.

Instagram: Post one time per day at different Instagram time.

Week 3:

Facebook: Post two to three times per day at non-peak times.

Instagram: Post one time per day in peak and non-peak times.

This strategy will help you to understand customer's engagement with the content at different hours. Track your results and work on creating new content by checking the demand of the audience.

Critical Thinking

All the big content marketers possess the skill of "critical thinking." An advertiser is always learning new tricks to create and promote unique material for their accounts on various social media platforms, you see. Nonetheless, not every tactic turns out to be successful.

To achieve success, you need a few skills to play with. Instead of sticking with techniques that do not work, you can think about a tactic critically and find possible ways to make it a huge success in the niche or situation that you are targeting. This job cannot last for a single day, and then you will decide that you should post it right away. Even if you have a great idea in mind, it still matters to improve it in any way you can.

Ask yourself this question: is this trick going to work or not? If yes, then what is needed to execute the idea? What possible options are available to implement it? Nobody is born with impeccable critical-thinking skills, but that is something that you can develop through practice. Make sure to brainstorm your ideas before putting them into your marketing strategies.

Content Length and Type

Let's talk about infographics here. Such materials with a minimum number of words gets extra attention from audience. This strategy works because it is easy to convert complex information into understandable infographics in less time and are more eye-catching for the audience.

Track Facebook and Instagram Insights

What do you do after a marketing campaign ends? Do you extract any information from the results that can used for future ads or not?

As en efficient social media marketer, it is your responsibility to do the latter after the conclusion of every marketing campaign. This will help you pinpoint potential key takeaways from each one of them, which you can use in future campaigns. The insights from the promoted ad campaigns can add up to your future strategies, you see. They provide all the necessary and detailed information about your social media engagement, likes, impressions, and shares. The data provided by Facebook and Instagram, to be specific, can work like a charm for social media marketers if analyzed properly. Make sure to keep track of what's working and what's not on these channels.

The Power of Data on Social Media Platforms

You can easily track weekly interactions, reach, views and impressions of the audience. The content tab also allows you to check how your stories and promotions are performing. The audience tab provides important insights into how users react to your posts.

What are Analytics?

It is the social media data that is the collected information from networks, which show how users share, view or engage with the content on your page. Some of its important aspects consist of:

- Shares

- Likes

- URL clicks

- Mentions

- New followers

- Impressions

- Comments

- Hashtag usage

- Keyword analysis

- Demographics

Your main focus should be on paid strategy. It also matters to experiment with different content and focus on page growth.

Benefits of Instagram Analytics

Instagram Insights are divided into two sections. One is focused on individual posts, while the other shows data on your profile as a whole.

Account Impressions - It refers to the number of times the posts and stories that got viewed by the audience.

Total Reach - This part tracks how many unique accounts viewed your posts and stories.

Website Clicks - This tab shows the number of clicks on your bio link.

Profile Visits - It refers to the number of clicks that your account page got.

Post Likes - This section shows the number of total likes received by a particular post.

Post Comments - It reveals the number of comments accumulated.

Posts Saved - It tracks how many unique accounts saved your post.

Follows - This tells you how many accounts started following your page over a period of time.

Benefits of Facebook Analytics

For those who own a Facebook business page, the most essential analytic metrics include:

Engagement - The number of post clicks, Likes, comments and shares happened in last week and that data is compared to the previous week.

Impressions - The number of times your Facebook Page is displayed, including audiences who clicked and did not click your brand's profile.

Organic Likes - The number of likes that did not come from a paid ad campaign.

Page Likes - This metric shows the total number of page likes that a post has garnered.

Paid Likes - It refers to the likes that you got through a paid ad campaign.

Post Reach - It shows the number of people who have seen and clicked any content or ads related to your page.

Reactions - This shows post reactions, including like, love, smiley, sad, wow, and angry.

Unlikes - The number of people who unliked your Facebook Page.

What we have learned from it and our strategy for the future is that there are ways to leverage Facebook and Instagram analytics and grow your brand following. After getting the analytics department of the platforms to report information regarding the activities in your accounts, you can use them to improve growth ideas.

Determine the Time When Your Audience Is Most Active

The best time to post a blog, image or video is when your audience is most active on social media platforms. You can find this data in the follower's Insights section, which is organized by day of the week and time of day. Using this report, make a proper strategy to post your content within the suitable time frames.

Demographics of the Audience

Focus on information related to the location, gender, and age of your target market. These things must be aligned with your objectives as a brand owner. Then, you may develop your content accordingly to attract the attention of the right segment of your audience.

Types of Content

Post relevant content that followers are interested in. You can use the posts section to know about the engagement, impressions, and reach data for your Instagram and Facebook stories, photos, and videos. You can also divide these three content types to know which tends to generate the best results.

Analyze Call to Action (CTA)

If you are using Instagram Insights, it is ideal to analyze whether your CTA is working or not. For instance, you have seen "click the link in the bio for more information" displayed on many accounts. It checks the traffic generated and can tell you how many people clicked the link that you have provided in your About page over the last several days. This information can help you keep an eye on the website or call clicks that have occurred on your profile.

An engaging and consistent presence on Instagram and Facebook platforms can attract more followers within your target market as time flows. So, have a little fun with getting to know these channels. Make an effort and be more focused on the time. Join conversations and interact with audiences from all around the globe as well. For example, you can participate in #MothersDay or #InternationalWomensDay on social media, as well as contribute meaningful posts that have a connection to a specific event. After that, you can measure impressions and engagement on these posts. Always explore new dimensions and try to experiment with the call-to-action buttons, too.

The world around us moves extremely fast, and it provides us an opportunity to sample different things on social media. For instance, you can test unique content vs. infographics. Also, you may keep tabs on brands to find out what trends are present on their channel and what content ideas you can gain from them.

Incorporate Facebook and Instagram

Social media is a very valuable tool for the promotion of your marketing content. The simplest way to expand your brand or business is to embed your strategies in Facebook and Instagram. This move will create a combined feed of your activities on both platforms.

In comparison with other social media sites, Facebook provides a plug-in generator that allows you to embed your feed on your website. Instagram does not have a plug-in generator like Facebook. In truth, the latter merely offers instructions regarding embedding an individual post.

A recent study generated these results and revealed that after the merger of Facebook and Instagram, Instagram was proven be more useful for generating traffic and increasing brands' sales.[38] Embedding social media profiles on your website will help to verify your web presence and boost interactions with the audience as well. It will ensure that valuable customers are aware of your online engagement.

Since Instagram and Facebook have the same ownership, it is easy and possible to link these two powerhouse platforms together.

Making the Most Out of These Social Media Platforms

Linking Instagram to Facebook to build brand awareness among the audience will result in increased customer reach. If you want excellent news for your business, you must consider what type of content to market your brand with to get the exposure that it deserves.

How Are Facebook and Instagram Different?

Instagram is purely a visual platform for the audience that involves engaging captions on pictures to capture a digital user's attention. Facebook is slightly different as it focuses more on text posts and articles.

---

[38] Luckerson, V. (2016). Here's proof that Instagram was one of the smartest acquisitions ever. Retrieved from http://time.com/4299297/instagram-facebook-revenue/

Integrating them together is quite effortless. Truth be told, it is also beneficial for your business growth. It has offered amazing results to multiple businesses already, so it's highly likely that your brand will meet the same fate on Facebook and Instagram, too.

Benefits of Using the Platforms Together

These days, people respond more to visual images; that's why linking Instagram and Facebook to each other will make it easy to share such content with your audiences. Using photos and videos is a great way to promote the character of your brand, and a well-established and trustworthy relationship is built between your business and the customer afterward. Small entrepreneurs can avail the full advantage of social media. In this competitive climate, these two social media platforms embedded together will make your brand look professional and easy to reach.

What Is It for?

Studies show that audience is happier to engage with the brands they follow than the ones that they don't. It enables you to promote your brand or business on both platforms together and build up your presence in the market, brand information, and engagement on your posts.

How Can You Create One Feed for Instagram and Facebook?

As Facebook took over Instagram, the latter acts as an extension of Facebook. When you embed Instagram with your Facebook account, the information provided is cross-checked directly. To be precise, it assesses the selected industry on which your page was created.

Advertise on Both Platforms

Using a business profile, Facebook allows you to choose where you want your ads to be placed, and one of those areas is Instagram. Ultimately, business profiles allow a better marketing experience for building a consistent following and engagement.

Pictures and Content Speak Louder Than Everything Else

Brands must be posting high-resolution images with the best supporting captions on social media platforms because this combo can speak to consumers in a thousand ways. People respond to visuals more than just simple text, you see. And when you link these two platforms, sharing the photos becomes easier and engagement increases with the audience, especially with your potential clients.

Build Credibility and Reliability

It is easy to get started and gain amazing results when you prioritize creating images with captions to promote your brand. Not only is it easily manageable but it also incorporates brand development and awareness, audience reach, more exposure, likes and comments, and other money-making opportunities.

The Unstoppable Shoppable Instagram

The first question that arises at this point is: how often do people visit your social media platform?

We are talking about Instagram here. Daily active users of this platform are 800 million, and 80% of all Instagram accounts follow a business profile.[39] In fact, users who find new products through this platform are 60%, and 75% of them take action after viewing a specific post.

As you know, you can create a catalog of products on Facebook and sell them via Instagram. For this purpose, the Facebook page must be connected to your Instagram business profile. When products are added to your Facebook catalog, it will automatically sync with Instagram and allow you to share shoppable posts.

After that, you will be able to run ads on the Instagram platform and share any advertisement that is originally on your Facebook account. You can also add filters, such as price range, gender, category, and online presence to reach a wider range.

Do you know what shoppable Instagram Stories are?

Instagrammers, they love to shop!

Instagram has added click-to-shop tags that are used in the stories and feed and in making it a lot easier than ever. It can be a clothing image, a product name with a sticker or a transparent text. (Users can swipe the product screen to view their full details.)

The whole concept depends upon this question: what Instagram shopping looks like, and what does it mean for you and your business?

Below are three ways to make your Instagram unstoppably shoppable.

Story Ads

_____

[39] Osman, M. (2018). 18 Instagram stats every marketer should know for 2018 [Blog Post]. Retrieved from https://sproutsocial.com/insights/instagram-stats/

"Stories" - this feature is available on Instagram and is used by businesses to throw ads in front of their potential customers. Users can see stories on the top of their feed. By selecting "Instagram Stories" as the location for posting ads, 400 million daily Instagram users will be getting your ad in a matter of seconds.[40]

Shoppable Posts

These are also known as shoppable tags. Instagram allows retailers to market their products with this tag, you see, and apply them directly in their posts. It provides information about the product name and price. Users can click on that tag, and it will take people towards making a purchase. In the past, you have to post "click on the link in our bio"; with this tag button available now, however, you can go straight to the product details.

Swipe-Up Links

This is a final and very user-friendly link for everyone. You just have to do one swipe, and you can get redirected to the website page through an Instagram story. More traffic is generated on the sites through this link since consumers can buy what they need without wasting a lot of time.

How to Make an Instagram Post Shoppable Using the Three Ways Mentioned Above

1. Upload the image you are using

Select and add an image to Instagram. Now, you can edit and add filters before uploading it.

2. Tag the products you have used in the image

Click on the tag option to tag a specific product that you have used in the image. Product-tagged images have a very good impact on customer's buying behavior because they find goods and accounts information together in one place.

3. Write your content

It is all about writing good content in the caption area with all the necessary information about the product. An expertly written description can be highly engaging and may turn into sales in a couple of clicks.

---

[40] Hutchinson, A. (2018). Instagram Stories now has 400 million daily active users. Retrieved from https://www.socialmediatoday.com/news/instagram-stories-now-has-400-million-daily-active-users/526818/

Final Thoughts

Using these tricks and techniques, you can make your business unstoppable. As a marketer, you need to keep up with the latest trends and make perfectly smart decisions based on what you see around your social media world.

Don't Buy Followers. I Repeat, Don't Even Think About It.

Instagram is the preferred and most favorite social platform of most top influencers. In recent years, Instagram has become a basic marketing and advertising network for many brands that not only want to compete with rivals but also hope to gain a huge following through Instagram. While it can be profitable for your business, it may waste the time and money that you have been investing as well. Perhaps you have been thinking of the former because top influencers earn nearly $18,000 per post. Nevertheless, Instagram has recently removed a huge number of fake followers from top influencers' platforms. So, if you have plans of buying Instagram likes and followers to fool your customers as a part of your Instagram strategy, you must rethink this approach.

Why Top Brands and Influencers Buy Instagram Likes and Followers

There are hundreds of different websites and pages that are selling promising likes and followers. User engagement is a very important factor to increase your post's popularity. To be on top of feeds, some folks assume that this scheme is necessary. However, only sharing an image and collecting likes and followers to capture people's attention should not be the ultimate goal. You better post engaging content, interact with people, and memorize proper hashtags to be able to keep your audience.

Fake following is being created because they are managed by users whose only goal is to get followed in return. Instagram is monitoring your fake followers, and it is deleting such accounts continuously. Thus, you may end up losing a lot of paid followers, and your Instagram account might suffer.

Issues That Occur After Buying Instagram Followers

If you use shortcuts, there is a risk of being banned by Instagram because of their strict policies. Audience nowadays is very smart, too; if they see that you have a high number of followers on your account but limited engagement, it is going to destroy your brand reputation.

How to Avoid Getting Banned on Instagram

The best way to avoid a ban is to post engaging content on daily and use the important hashtags related to your product. Audience engagement plays a huge role in the success of any brand; that's why you should not do anything to anger them.

1. Remember that your follower's engagement is a reflection of your brand

Most of the social media users who actually want to make a purchase from your brand will make sure that your account is real by going through your follower's list and content. If you have too many accounts that turned out to be fake, it will cause the audience to go away.

2. Build a genuine relationship with your audience

Be true to yourself and your brand. If you work hard on your content and image building, organically speaking, your following is going to get genuine likes and followers.

3. Keep in mind that fake likes will never equal to real business

No matter how many likes your posts get or even if your brand is so popular, paid engagements never result to real business.

How to Gain Likes on Instagram Naturally

Paid following is not everything.

How many people show engagement with your brand on a regular basis? How much traffic is coming on your website through your social efforts?

Stop looking at the number of followers that you have. Instead, look at the things that matter, including engaging content.

Pro Tip: If you use unique hashtags for your brand, especially formatted bio, play with your platform's algorithm, like and comments on other users account, use GIF images, and get featured by other accounts to garner unique and genuine following. You can also contact social media experts; they will help you build your presence on digital platforms.

Conclusion

Social media marketing allow brands to promote their products and services to potential users on different platforms. The digital networking sites such as Facebook and Instagram offer numerous advertising options to marketers. It is their responsibility to evaluate different factors and make the right combination of ideas for their businesses. We have discussed different aspects of social media marketing in the previous chapters, as well as how brands can adopt proven strategies to increase their brand awareness and user engagement.

This book has provided a complete walkthrough towards social media marketing tactics and strategies that may allow any brand to succeed advertising their products and services on various channels. When we talk about social media, we must mention the fact that it promises positive outcomes for businesses as it gives them a platform to grow in the competitive market.

As we know, there are more than 1.5 billion social network users available worldwide, and seven out of ten individuals are active on prominent social media platforms like Facebook and Instagram.[41] Over the last few years, many countries have seen a huge rise in smartphone usage. A consumer with internet access on smartphones uses social platforms more intensively, and so the latter have become a massive part of all our lives. Social media has gained so much growth that it is now easy to connect with people, brands, and businesses that ultimately transform users into potential customers.

Because of their popularity, many researchers are now interested in learning how these social platforms are affecting our community and what new trends are there to be followed. People from different age groups can stay connected through these sites, you see. Sitting behind a computer and communicating with people from all around the world has become a routine for big brands through this interactive media. Companies also interact with the potential customers almost every day by posting interactive and eye-catching content on their social media pages, through user-focused email, et cetera. Users wants to be involved and engaged with brands as well, and so they participate in different surveys and competitions offered by companies with an aim to help them improve their existing products and services.

Social media marketing has become a necessity for brands and businesses because it depicts their overall presence and brand image in the market, as well as their impact on

---

[41] Pew Research Center. (2018). Social media fact sheet. Retrieved from https://www.pewinternet.org/fact-sheet/social-media/

the users. There are also numerous techniques available to boost their social media presence. Active internet users spend 142 minutes of their day on these social networks.[42] That is why business world run by the marketers focus on social media and marketing using different platforms. 60% of them claim to have acquired new customers through social networks, and so the implementation of these strategies has become a part of business practice.

Social media are available in different forms and offer diverse functionalities for every platform. Keeping track of different social media networking sites can help us to better understand the available ways of marketing that businesses can use to organize their online presence. An established business practice creates a team of social experts to control their profiles. We have seen that their responsibility ranges from creating attractive content to engaging with the online audience by answering queries and replying to feedback.

We have also covered specific topics in the book, such as how brand that runs multiple social media accounts for their brand recognition and awareness can explore some of the new and unique trends and use them efficiently to achieve success. Additionally, if utilized smartly, they will be able to create a pool of potential customers, which they can target for later product announcements, sales, and interactions.

Most brand-related content posted by the influencers or audiences can be seen on Facebook and Instagram. The engagement rate of these two social media platforms can be seen in details above. An audience is much quicker to post brand content on Instagram as compared to Facebook. In the long run, we can say from the comparison that Instagram may well develop into a very interesting platform for brand promotion. The social media marketing trends keep on changing; thus, it is important for brands to remain on top of their game all the time.

---

[42] Salim, S. (2019). How much time do you spend on social media? Research says 142 minutes per day. Retrieved from https://www.digitalinformationworld.com/2019/01/how-much-time-do-people-spend-social-media-infographic.html

References

Adobe Digital Insights. (2018). State of digital advertising [Slideshow]. Retrieved from https://www.slideshare.net/adobe/adi-state-of-digital-advertising-2018

Collins, A. (n.d.). Instagram marketing: The ultimate guide. Retrieved from https://www.hubspot.com/instagram-marketing

Constine, J. (2018). Facebook Stories: The complete guide for businesses in 2019. Retrieved from https://www.oberlo.com/blog/facebook-stories-guide

da Chunha, M. (2019). The complete guide to advertising on Instagram. Retrieved from https://www.wordstream.com/blog/ws/2017/11/20/instagram-advertising

Doeing, D. (2018). 58 powerful video marketing statistics for 2019. Retrieved from https://learn.g2crowd.com/video-marketing-statistics

Enge, E. (2018). Mobile vs desktop usage in 2018: Mobile widens the gap. Retrieved from https://www.stonetemple.com/mobile-vs-desktop-usage-study/

Facebook Business. (n.d.). Carousel ads. Retrieved from https://www.facebook.com/business/ads/carousel-ad-format?ref=ens_rdr

Facebook Business. (2018). Sephora. Retrieved from https://www.facebook.com/business/success/2-sephora

Facebook Business. (2015). The value of video for brands. Retrieved from https://en-gb.facebook.com/business/news/insights/the-value-of-video-for-brands

Finn, A. (2018). Facebook Ads Manager vs Power Editor: Which is better?. Retrieved from https://www.wordstream.com/blog/ws/2017/08/22/facebook-ads-manager-vs-power-editor

Fishman, E. (2016). How long should your next video be? Retrieved from https://wistia.com/learn/marketing/optimal-video-length

Harrison, K. (n.d.). Audience segmentation is important for better communication [Blog Post]. Retrieved from https://cuttingedgepr.com/free-articles/core-pr-skills/audience-segmentation-important-better-communication/

Hobson, N. (2018). The science of FOMO and what we're really missing out on. Retrieved from https://www.psychologytoday.com/us/blog/ritual-and-the-brain/201804/the-science-fomo-and-what-we-re-really-missing-out

Hutchinson, A. (2018). Facebook rolls out group stories to all regions. Retrieved from https://www.socialmediatoday.com/news/facebook-rolls-out-group-stories-to-all-regions/543562/

Hutchinson, A. (2018). Instagram Stories now has 400 million daily active users. Retrieved from https://www.socialmediatoday.com/news/instagram-stories-now-has-400-million-daily-active-users/526818/

Imgur. (2015). Humans are changing: How to adapt your brand [Infographic]. Retrieved from https://imgur.com/468Awwl

Jones, B. (2016). In video advertising, Is longer stronger? Retrieved from https://www.thinkwithgoogle.com/consumer-insights/unskippable-video-advertising-ad-recall-brand-favorability/

Kant, V. & Xu, J. (2016). Taking into account live video when ranking feed. Retrieved from https://newsroom.fb.com/news/2016/03/news-feed-fyi-taking-into-account-live-video-when-ranking-feed/

Karlson, K. (2019). Facebook ads A/B testing in 2019 – Why, what, and how to split test. Retrieved from https://karolakarlson.com/facebook-ad-ab-testing-rules/

Kolowich, L. (2017). 16 video marketing statistics to inform your 2019 strategy [Infographic]. Retrieved from https://blog.hubspot.com/marketing/video-marketing-statistics

Launchway Media. (2018). 16 statistics that prove personalized content works [Blog Post]. Retrieved from https://www.launchwaymedia.com/blog/2018/5/14/16-statistics-that-prove-personalized-content-works

Linqia. (2017). The value of influencer content 2017 [PDF File]. Retrieved from http://www.linqia.com/wp-content/uploads/2017/04/The-Value-of-Influencer-Content-2017_Final_Report.pdf

Logan, B. (2009). 200 million strong [Blog Post]. Retrieved from https://www.facebook.com/notes/facebook/200-million-strong/72353897130/

Luckerson, V. (2016). Here's proof that Instagram was one of the smartest acquisitions ever. Retrieved from http://time.com/4299297/instagram-facebook-revenue/

Marketing Charts. (2018). So people want brands to be more transparent on social media. What does that mean? Retrieved from https://www.marketingcharts.com/brand-related-105434

Mawhinney, J. (2019). 45 visual content marketing statistics you should know in 2019.

Retrieved from https://blog.hubspot.com/marketing/visual-content-marketing-strategy

Newberry, C. (2018). Social media advertising 101: How to get the most out of your budget. Retrieved from https://blog.hootsuite.com/social-media-advertising/

Nike. (2019). Nike - Dream Crazier [Video File]. Retrieved from https://www.youtube.com/watch?v=whpJ19RJ4JY

Osman, M. (2018). 18 Instagram stats every marketer should know for 2018 [Blog Post]. Retrieved from https://sproutsocial.com/insights/instagram-stats/

Page, M. (2018). How to create a Facebook Instant Experience ad (previously canvas ads). Retrieved from https://thedigiterati.com/how-to-create-a-facebook-canvas-ad-now-known-as-instant-experiences/

Patel, N. (n.d.). The marketer's guide to Instagram Stories: Building Your brand and generating sales [Blog Post]. Retrieved from https://neilpatel.com/blog/marketers-guide-to-instagram-stories/

Peterson, T. (2017). Facebook's shoppable 'Collection' ad is its latest iAd-like format. Retrieved from https://marketingland.com/facebooks-shoppable-collection-ad-latest-iad-like-format-209886

Petruca, I. (2016). Personal branding through social media [PDF File]. Retrieved from http://ijcr.eu/articole/345_10%20Irina%20PETRUCA.pdf

Pew Research Center. (2018). Social media fact sheet. Retrieved from https://www.pewinternet.org/fact-sheet/social-media/

Phelan, D. (2018). Why IGTV is Instagram's bravest update yet: Longer video app to take on YouTube (Updated). Retrieved from https://www.forbes.com/sites/davidphelan/2018/06/21/instagram-reveals-igtv-dedicated-hub-and-new-app-for-much-longer-videos/

Salim, S. (2019). How much time do you spend on social media? Research says 142 minutes per day. Retrieved from https://www.digitalinformationworld.com/2019/01/how-much-time-do-people-spend-social-media-infographic.html

Sprout Social. (n.d.). Social media & the evolution of transparency. Retrieved from https://sproutsocial.com/insights/guides/

Statista. (n.d.). Number of monthly active Facebook users worldwide as of 4th quarter 2018 (in millions). Retrieved from https://www.statista.com/statistics/264810/number-of-monthly-active-facebook-users-worldwide/

Vrountas, T. (2018). The Facebook 20% rule: Why your ads might not be running. Retrieved from https://instapage.com/blog/facebook-20-text-rule

Wallace, T. (n.d.). [Infographic] Modern consumer behavior in the new omni-channel world + 31 expert tips to dominate it now. Retrieved from https://www.bigcommerce.com/blog/consumer-behavior-infographic/#31-experts-on-dominating-an-omnichannel-strategy

Weaver, B. (2018). Facebook Instant Experience ads: The new and improved canvas ads. Retrieved from https://instapage.com/blog/instant-experience-ads

Made in the USA
Columbia, SC
07 June 2019